UNSEEN HAZARDS

THAT THREATEN HUNTERS, CAMPERS, AND HIKERS:

WHAT YOU SHOULD KNOW ABOUT PATHOGENS COMMONLY FOUND IN WILDLIFE, INCLUDING

RABIES,

TETANUS (LOCKJAW),

TULAREMIA (RABBIT FEVER),

BRUCELLOSIS (UNDULANT FEVER),

ROCKY MOUNTAIN SPOTTED FEVER,

AND

BORRELIA (LYME DISEASE)

by

Jerry Genesio

Illustrations are reproduced with compliments of Microsoft; Clker.com of Germantown, MD; Public Domain Clip Art at pdclipart.org; and the Alaska Rural Systemic Initiative funded by the National Science Foundation Annenberg Rural Challenge.

To my children,

Louie, Lauri, Mark, and Kristy,

whose love of and appreciation for nature

have been inspirational.

- -

UNSEEN HAZARDS

Let children walk with Nature, let them see the beautiful blendings and communions of death and life, their joyous inseparable unity, as taught in woods and meadows, plains and mountains and streams of our blessed star, and they will learn that death is stingless indeed, and as beautiful as life.

John Muir

The superior man, when resting in safety, does not forget that danger may come. When in a state of security he does not forget the possibility of ruin. When all is orderly, he does not forget that disorder may come. Thus his person is not endangered, and his States and all their clans are preserved.

Confucius

INDEX

UNSEEN HAZARDS

INTRODUCTION

Zoonotic diseases are defined as those diseases that can be transmitted from animals to humans and from humans to animals, the latter sometimes called *reverse zoonotics*. There are some 150 zoonotic diseases that are known to exist, and many of these are known to infect wild animals. There is no reason to be alarmed or frightened, but everyone should be aware of these threats and use sensible preventive measures to avoid them, especially those who are most exposed. The zoonotic diseases described herein are a greater threat to those who enjoy and participate in outdoor activities such as hunting, camping, and hiking in particular.

Humans dominate this planet, but we also share it with many other forms of life. Some are familiar to us, such as plant and animal life; others not so much, like bacteria and viruses, or germs. The latter exist in the form of primitive, microscopic organisms that are very widely distributed throughout nature. Some are classified as *useful*. Without them, grazing animals such as cattle, sheep, and goats would be unable to digest the plant life they depend on for nourishment. We would be unable to produce gourmet delights like cheese, sauerkraut, or sour cream, but more importantly, we would be unable to produce antibiotics without which many thousands, perhaps even millions, of lives would be lost annually.

A second category of germs is made up of similar microorganisms that are presently considered essentially *harmless*. They're not especially beneficial, but conversely, they don't pose a threat to health or life either, as far as we know. These occur abundantly in the environment on and/or in plants, animals, and humans.

The third classification of bacteria and viruses includes those *known to be harmful.* Unfortunately, we're seldom aware that our body has been invaded by these tiny, foreign creatures until they've established enough of a foothold to have become a serious threat to our health, or perhaps even our life. They work silently. At best they may be debilitating, at worst they may be deadly. Some attack quickly, others may conceal themselves deep in the tissues of our bodies and lie dormant until one day, perhaps a year or more after entry, something, for some reason, awakens them. Then, like an angry grizzly, they thrash about in a rage, intent upon destruction, defiantly ignoring the cardinal rule of nature, self-survival, by feverishly attacking the one thing that provides them with life – their host.

Oddly enough there is a sub-class in this category of harmful bacteria and viruses which consists of those that are capable of either action, quick or delayed, depending on circumstances not yet fully understood. One such demon is the rabies virus.

RABIES

Once inside the body of a warm-blooded creature the rabies virus usually strikes within 60 days, but may remain dormant for up to a year or longer. On the other hand, it may mount a literally nerve-wracking and murderous attack within a week of entry.

The rabies virus has existed perhaps since life on earth began, and was considered by some to have been Satan's contribution to genesis. It was described nearly 4,000 years ago in the pre-Mosaic code of ancient Mesopotamia. Homer, writing in the 8th century B.C., portrayed its dramatic symptoms. Democritus and Aristotle were at least acquainted with it in the 4th and 3rd centuries B.C. A method of treatment is offered in the Babylonian Talmud, circa 500 A.D., whereby patients were instructed to drink only from a copper tube "lest he see the shadow of the demon and be endangered." It was apparently thought that the fear of water, or hydrophobia, which often accompanies the disease, was caused by the reflection in the water of the drinker's own madness.

In the early years of America's colonization the cry of "Mad Dog" sent women scurrying for their children, and men for their weapons. It was well known that a rabid bite meant certain death. It was not known why, but the knowledge of how death was visited upon the victim struck terror into human hearts.

During the early or *prodromal* stage following a non-specific period of incubation or dormancy, the victim characteristically develops a high fever (102° F. more or less). There is nausea and vomiting, headache, general malaise, increased fatigability, loss of appetite, sore throat, cough, depression, and restlessness. Unusual sensations of pain, tingling, and burning begin near the site of exposure. This may last from one to four days before the second or *encephalitic* stage begins signaled by excessive restlessness and increasing to uncontrollable excitement. The victim becomes confused, hallucinatory, even combative. Bizarre aberrations of thought predominate; muscles spasm; the body assumes an arched, prone posture supported only by the feet and the head; seizures and focal paralysis ensue. The fever often rises to 105° F. or higher, the sense of touch becomes excruciatingly painful, hypersensitivity to bright light, loud noises, even air disturbances, becomes intolerable. Tears, perspiration, and saliva flow.

The third stage is referred to as that of *dysfunction.* There is double vision, facial palsies, and foaming at the mouth in classical madness. Extreme thirst but painful or total inability to swallow causes the victim to avoid water. Finally there is complete paralysis, coma, and death. This horrifying scenario may span four to six days and accurately describes what is called *furious* rabies, the most frequent type encountered. Occasionally a victim will suffer *dumb* rabies, named thusly because the paralysis immediately affects the voice muscles, and speech is reduced severely or rendered impossible. In these instances death may result sooner from paralysis of the breathing apparatus. The latter has been noted most frequently, but not exclusively, following rabid bites by vampire bats.

Until recent scientific developments in the early 1970s, a diagnosis of rabies invariably meant certain death. In 1968 a team, led by the internationally known virologist Dr. Victor J.

Cabasso, began experimenting with a new treatment for rabies. Four years later they met with success. They were not pioneers however, for nearly a century earlier, in 1884, Louis Pasteur discovered a preventive vaccine for rabies, and if it was administered immediately and the dormancy period was long enough, it was usually effective, otherwise, it was useless. On occasion severe and sometimes fatal reactions resulted from the vaccine itself, but there was little choice in the matter.

Today we have much less dangerous vaccines that can be given in conjunction with Dr. Cabasso's treatment, if necessary, which involves the injection of previously developed rabies antibodies. Suffice it to say that the anxiety and abject fear of rabies infection is not what it was less than a few decades ago. Professional advice and early treatment, however, remain essential. Even today those who survive diagnosed rabies have suffered permanent damage to nerve and brain tissue, new treatments notwithstanding.

Large scale campaigns to vaccinate domestic animals have resulted in steadily declining incidences in this category. The 6,200 cases in 1953 compare favorably with only 547 in 2006. Now, in the United States, wild animals are the largest source of infection-threat for human beings. Of 6,943 laboratory confirmed cases in 2006, 92% occurred in wild animals and only 8% in the domestic variety. In the wild category the major hosts were raccoons (38%), bats (24%), skunks (22%), foxes (6%), and other (2%). The *other* category includes 66 mongoose (all in Puerto Rico), 43 groundhogs, 30 bobcats, 10 coyotes, 6 deer, 4 otters, 2 opossums, and 1 each rabbit, cougar, wolf hybrid, and fisher.

According to the Southeastern Cooperative Wildlife Disease Study (SCWDS), "Rabies is extremely rare in white-tailed deer, with 0-2 cases reported annually from 1980-1990 in the United States. Only one deer in over 800 submitted to the SCWDS diagnostic laboratory has been infected, and this animal had raccoon-strain virus. The highest incidence of rabies in deer occurred in 1991 when eight cases were reported, seven of which were in New Jersey, New York, and Maryland. This apparent rise may reflect the increased incidence of rabies in the northeastern United States, or may only be an artifact of increased public awareness. Rabid deer may display abnormal behavior ranging from severe depression to violent aggression, or they may appear uncoordinated, partially paralyzed, or unable to rise." SCWDS, based at the University of Geogia's College of Veterinary Medicine in Athens, GA., publishes *SCWDS Briefs,* a quarterly newsletter that can be accessed online at http://www.uga.edu/scwds/briefs.htm .

The New York State Department of Health's Wadsworth Center (WC) reported that rabies was confirmed in 20 deer in the state during 1993 "including 18 wild white-tailed deer and two captive Sika deer (farm-bred for meat)." Of 272 white-tailed deer submitted that year, 76 had demonstrated signs of illness suggestive of rabies: "of these 18 were rabid." All of these cases occurred in areas where raccoon rabies was known to be present. The WC identified five rabid deer in 1992, and only three in 1991.

Between 1992 and 2001 the WC also diagnosed rabies in seven rabbits. Of these three had been exposed to raccoons and one had been exposed to a skunk. All seven infected rabbits had the raccoon variant of the virus. Clinical signs in these rabbits included paralysis (the most common clinical sign), mild hypersalivation, biting the air, lethargy, anorexia, and death.

In 2006, 49 states, Puerto Rico, and the District of Columbia reported cases of rabies-infected animals. Only Hawaii remains consistently rabies-free. Rabies in humans has declined proportionately. In the 14-year period preceding 1960, there was an average of 22 cases per year compared to a low of zero and a high of six per year since then. *"Although Rabies in humans is rare in the United States, every year approximately 16,000-39,000 persons receive post-exposure prophylaxis"*, according to the Centers for Disease Control and Prevention (CDC) in Atlanta, GA.

Initially it was thought that the rabies virus could only be transmitted through a bite wound. Recent discoveries have established, however, that infection can result if a rabid, but not necessarily symptomatic, animal merely licks a scratch, abrasion, open wound, or even mucous membrane tissue such as that in the vicinity of the eyes, the mouth, and the genitals. This is a fact of paramount significance when wild or non-vaccinated domestic animals are in contact with, or have easy access to, young children. Even transmission through the air via the respiratory tract is now known to be possible and has occurred in the bat caves of Texas.

Inside the host, the rabies virus, sooner or later, seeks to make contact with nerve tissue. Once this is achieved it travels along the neural pathway toward the central nervous system. Eventually it passes centrifugally along the nervous system to the glands and vital organs, most notably the salivary glands, adrenal medulla (a gland near the kidney which produces hormones essential to life), kidney, brain, and heart.

Rationale of treatment for rabies today involves answers to several key questions.

- *Has the animal's saliva entered the subject's body?* If the subject has not been bitten, scratched or licked on an open wound or mucous membrane, there is very little risk.

- *What was the vaccination status of the animal?* The chances of contracting rabies from a properly vaccinated animal are minimal; however, if the animal's behavior is not normal, professional advice should be sought.

- *Is the animal likely to be rabid?* Carnivorous animals (especially raccoons, skunks, foxes, dogs, and cats) and bats are more likely to be rabid than non-carnivorous animals.

- *Was the animal provoked?* Most wild animals avoid contact with people. Therefore, any wild animal that bites a person should be considered rabid. Any bite inflicted while attempting to handle or feed an apparently healthy domestic animal should generally be regarded as provoked. A normally friendly domestic animal that bites, without apparent provocation, should be considered suspect.

Management of a suspect animal depends on whether it is wild or domestic. Any wild animal that bites or scratches a person should be killed at once and its head shipped under refrigeration to a qualified laboratory for examination. A physician and a veterinarian should be contacted for assistance. Most local and all state health departments also offer qualified help in such instances.

Bites inflicted by apparently healthy domestic animals, because of their domesticity and likelihood of having been vaccinated, are less threatening. Nevertheless, the animal should be confined and observed by a veterinarian for *10 days*. If it shows signs during that period indicating that it may be rabid, it should be sacrificed and its brain examined. Of course, permission must first be obtained from the animal's owner or from public health authorities.

Persons suspected of having been exposed to rabies should seek professional advice immediately. *A delay of 24 hours has proven fatal.* In the case of unknown, unnaturally acting, or escaped wild or domestic animals, exposure to rabies must be assumed by the layman and thoroughly investigated by professionals.

A case of human rabies reported in 1979 involved a 50 year-old victim from Wheeling, West Virginia, who died on January 4, 1979. No clear source of rabies in this case has been identified. He was a carpenter by trade, and had gone deer hunting the previous November. If he had been exposed to a lick, or a bite, by any wild or domestic animal, he had never mentioned it to anyone. The cause of his death was officially determined by post-mortem autopsy resulting in

166 people, in two states, reasonably judged to have had exposure, being prophylactically treated for rabies.

Rabies is a merciless killer. For optimum protection domestic animals should be vaccinated at proper intervals; wild animals, even the cute, young and apparently defenseless ones, should be left in their natural environment; and maximum safety precautions should be taken by outdoorsmen when handling dead or dying animals, such as wearing gloves and avoiding contact with saliva.

TETANUS (LOCKJAW)

Tetanus, more commonly referred to even today as *Lockjaw,* is caused by a spindle or rod shaped microorganism of usually no more than .3 to .5 microns in length. Laid end to end, 5,000 of them would measure less than one inch. They are of the *Clostridium* genus, from the Greek word *kloster* for spindle, and belong to the *Bacillaceae* family of bacteria. *Clostridia* are anaerobic, meaning they live without air. In fact, oxygen actually threatens their survival, causing them to shun it much like nocturnal prowlers avoid the light of day. These spore-forming rods are widely distributed in nature; common in the soil and in the intestinal tracts of humans and animals. They are hardy, having a phenomenal resistance to drying, heating, and antiseptic agents, and pose special difficulty for the sterilization of instruments and the cleansing of wounds. This resistance accounts for their ability to survive in soil and dust under practically any condition. Lockjaw, more specifically, is caused by the microorganism *Clostridium Tetani,* hence the term *tetanus.*

Dirty wounds have long been considered potential hosts for *C. Tetani,* particularly if received in or near a barnyard. But, when we came to recognize the validity and significance of statistics and began stockpiling reliable data, we learned that *C. Tetani* was not so easily confined. The fact that automobile accident victims and war casualties were prime candidates for tetanus soon became evident. Recent studies indicate that

C. Tetani is virtually everywhere. According to some reports, the vast majority of tetanus-associated injuries are sustained in the home. Injuries involving lawn mowers are extremely tetanus prone. Tetanus cannot be ruled out, however, in those cases where the wound is not traumatic and deep. It is known to be associated with relatively minor lesions, and perhaps 20% of all cases occur without any identifiable injury or break in the skin, though at least some of these may be related to insect bites.

Unlike most bacteria and viruses, *C. Tetani* does not attack the human organism directly. It does, however, produce *Tetanospasmin,* one of the most lethal exotoxins (a poison excreted by a microorganism) known to science. Consequently, it may be said that tetanus is the result of intoxication, rather than infection; an intoxication strongly resembling that of strychnine poisoning with which, if there is no apparent injury, it may be confused until strychnine ingestion is ruled out. This exotoxin binds, rapidly and irreversibly, to nerve tissue and once bound cannot be neutralized. Treatment must focus on the neutralization of unbound Tetanospasmin and the prevention of further *Tetanospasmin* production. This exotoxin enters the central nervous system via peripheral motor nerves, or it may be blood borne. In its purified crystalline form it contains more than 20 million mouse-lethal doses per milligram. Time is of the essence. Fast and accurate diagnosis is the key to survival.

C. Tetani can survive for many years in or on dirt, wood, and a variety of other substances that we become involved with when camping, hunting, fishing, and participating in other outdoor activities. As it is commonly found in the intestines of animals, hunters should use caution when field dressing game, especially if they have open sores or lesions on their hands that would allow *C. Tetani* spores to enter their bodies. Usually the risk is even greater for those who are

55 years of age or older because they are less likely to have updated their tetanus vaccination. Deep wounds, such as those inflicted by an arrow or bullet, are the most dangerous because they are not easily cleaned properly.

Once having penetrated the human tissue mass, *C. Tetani* spores may germinate in from 1 to more than 21 days, usually 7 to 14 days. There appears to be a direct relationship between the incubation period and the rate of survival. If the incubation period is less than 10 days, the mortality rate is over 60%; if it is greater than 10 days, the odds of survival improve dramatically and the mortality rate progressively decreases to about 35%.

In view of the above, simple procedures such as wide exposure and flushing of a wound; removal of dirt or other foreign material; the cutting away of loose or dead tissue; administration of a tetanus toxoid booster; and, if the patient has been lax about immunization schedules, an injection of tetanus immune globulin (Human), are all considered *life-saving measures.*

The first signs of tetanus are usually stiffness of the jaw, throat, and neck muscles. Soon thereafter the jaw becomes fixed (lockjaw), the voice is altered, and facial muscles contract producing a wild, excited expression clinically referred to as *risus sardonicus.* Finally the muscles of the back and extremities convulse in spasm. Body temperature may reach 113° F. and continue to rise after death. Pain is intense and the mind is mercilessly clear and functional. When fatal, the patient usually expires from strangulation or from sheer exhaustion. Strangely enough however, if the patient should have the good fortune to recover, there is usually no permanent loss of muscle function. Another ironic feature of clinical tetanus is that victims may not become immune to the disease by virtue of having had it.

In the 19th century Arthur Nicolaier, a German physician, discovered the tetanus clostridium and proved that *C. Tetani* was present in the earth around us by producing the disease in animals injected with a solution containing common soil. Years later, in 1890, Japanese bacteriologist Shibasaburo Kitasato (1852-1931), and German physiologist Emil Adolph von Behring (1845-1917), working together at the Kock Institute in Berlin, produced an antitoxin that counteracted the effects of *Tetanospasmin*. Later Kitasato returned to Japan and established a private laboratory that eventually merged with the University of Tokyo. In 1901, von Behring was awarded the first Nobel Prize for Physiology and Medicine for his work in the field of immunology, particularly with regard to tetanus and diphtheria (both of the *Clostridium genus*).

Just prior to the turn of the last century and as a result of Kitasato's and von Behring's discoveries, Edmond Nocard (1850-1903) successfully immunized horses with an antitoxic horse serum and, though its use provided only a passive or short-lived immunity to tetanus, it saved many lives during World War I. Nocard, a French veterinarian, biologist, and once an assistant to the dean of bacteriology, Louis Pasteur, might never have concentrated on tetanus had it not been for the work of yet another European before him. Paul Ehrlich (1854-1915), a German bacteriologist and immunologist who shared the 1908 Nobel Prize, developed what has since been referred to as *Ehlich's side-chain theory.* This postulated that protoplasmic cells in the blood possess receptors, or *side-chains,* that are capable of detaching themselves from their mother cell and becoming fixed to certain protein cells with which they have an affinity. When this happens the original cell responds by producing more side-chains, which are again liberated into the blood where they may combine with more proteinic toxin cells and thereby render them inert. In effect, the result is the formation of free-floating antitoxin. Ehrlich's theory later resulted in the development of tetanus toxoid, which is *Tetanospasmin* treated so that its toxicity is destroyed but, when injected into the human body, it is still capable of inducing the formation of side-chains that will seek out and render toxic *Tetanospasmin* cells inert. In other words, tetanus toxoid will provide immunity, an active or long-term immunity, that will protect those vaccinated from the devastating results of *C. Tetani* invasion. Its value was established during World War II. All U.S. and British troops were vaccinated on induction into military service and tetanus toxoid proved so effective that, of the 1,076,245 U.S. troops wounded during the war, only eight developed tetanus.

Nevertheless, scientific research focusing on *C. Tetani* has been a frustrating mélange of successes unbalanced by residual failures. As previously noted, death from tetanus is, directly or indirectly, usually caused by extremely violent muscle spasms. Many years before Kitasato, von Behring, or Ehrlich were born it was known that certain South American Indian tribes dipped their arrow heads in a poison capable of inducing paralysis. It was called *curare* by the Spanish conquistadores, which literally meant *he, to whom it comes, falls*. Further investigation revealed that *curare* was no more than an extract from the *Chondrodendron* and *Strychnos* plants. (It is indeed ironic that an extract of the *Strychnos* plant might be used to treat tetanus while strychnine, also a *Strychnos* extract, produces symptoms that may result in a differential diagnosis.)

By 1811, curare was suggested for the treatment of tetanus, but trials proved that the dose required to eliminate the dreaded tetanus-related muscle spasms was unfortunately sufficient to paralyze the muscles required for ventilation. Where the affliction *could* result in death, the curare treatment in adequate dosage *always* resulted in death. Needless to say it was discontinued, but nearly 150 years later, in 1953, following the development of positive pressure ventilation through a tracheotomy tube introduced in Denmark, curare as a treatment for tetanus was resurrected for controlling convulsions and spasms, and as an adjunct for relaxing skeletal muscles in anesthesia. Tracheotomy and the administration of curare were once standard treatments for combating the symptoms of tetanus, but today synthetic, curare-like drugs, such as succinylcholine, have become more widely used and successful substitutes because they can be given in precise dosages with predictable effects.

The road to understanding and successfully treating tetanus was a long one cluttered with pitfalls. While vaccination with tetanus toxoid will provide active or long-term immunity, it will not do so immediately. Its protective shield, so to speak, does not develop swiftly enough to provide protection against lethal volumes of *Tetanospasmin* that can be produced by *C. Tetani* already present in the human body.

Physicians examining accident victims with open wounds must consider tetanus as a potential complication. For many years refined strains of Nocard's horse serum antitoxin were the only available means of providing immediate, if short-lived (passive), immunity. This protected the patient until either an initial or booster toxoid vaccination had sufficient time to take, causing Ehrlich's side-chains to form. However, the horse serum injection, like curare, all too frequently created problems more life-threatening than those posed by *C. Tetani,* which in the vast majority of cases may not have even been present.

Horse serum, or certain proteins contained in it, may be recognized by individual immunological systems as foreign. In patients with a hypersensitivity to certain types of foreign proteins, manifestations of allergy ranging from a rash to an anaphylactic reaction (shock resulting from physical rejection) may occur. It is often seen in patients who are hypersensitive to wasp or bee venom. Estimates of the frequency of these reactions following injection of tetanus antitoxin of equine origin vary from 5% to 30%. In all cases where horse serum antitoxin was indicated, physicians had to weigh the advantages against the disadvantages and always carefully scrutinize the patient's medical history for previous incidents where horse serum was or was likely to have been injected, possibly sensitizing the patient and setting the stage for anaphylactic shock.

Only within the last half-century, beginning in the early 1960s, has an antitoxin of human origin (tetanus immune globulin, Human) been widely available. Derived, or fractionated, from human blood plasma, sensitization to repeated injections of human immune globulin is extremely rare.

According to Dr. Daniel Dire of the University of Texas at Houston, the annual incidence of tetanus worldwide is greater than 500,000. Each year about 180,000 newborn babies die from neonatal tetanus. In some African nations and in the West Indies, dung is still occasionally used by some midwives as a dressing for the umbilical stump of newborns. Maternal tetanus also takes the lives of about 30,000 mothers every year and is responsible for the death of at least one in every 20 mothers. Even so, education and hygiene have played major roles in reducing the global incidence rate.

TETANUS (LOCKJAW)

In the 1950s there was an average of 500 cases of tetanus in the United States annually, but that figure has declined significantly. Of 130 cases reported in the United States from 1998-2000 (an average of 43 per year), California and Texas, with 35 and 16 respectively, had the highest reported number of cases.

With regard to societal segments, no group or individual is so privileged as to be exempt from accidents or the consequent threat posed by *C. Tetani.* At the other extreme, tetanus has become more common among drug addicts.

Generally, *C. Tetani* makes no class distinctions and continues to find receptive hosts in every part of the world regardless of climate, season, or social status. Individual susceptibility statistics have proven only that it is, typically, a bully of tyrannical torment preferring the weakest among us while testing indiscriminately as opportunities arise. Strength to ward off this natural enemy of humankind, even for the feeble, may be gained through immunization, but in keeping with current recommendations, immunization is imperative for the safety of all regardless of physical vitality.

TULAREMIA (RABBIT FEVER)

Each year hundreds of Vermonters trek along the thousands of miles of creeks and rivers in the state's three watershed areas trapping muskrats. The most popular time is late March to early April when melting ice and snow flood the animals out of their burrows. The year 1968 was different in only one respect; trappers working the Lake Champlain Watershed were unknowingly exposing themselves to an unseen competitor, and a menace to humankind. Within a four week period 47 people from 11 to 82 years of age who had either trapped or handled muskrats in Addison County, Vermont, fell ill, some very seriously. An investigation led by the Vermont State Health Department in cooperation with the National Communicable Disease Center determined that the sickness was tularemia.

Officials were shocked. Vermont was the only one of the 49 continental states that had never previously reported a case of tularemia. During the previous decade, most cases had been from states west of the Mississippi River – Arkansas, Louisiana, Oklahoma, and Texas – and these four occasionally reported half of the yearly total of human tularemia infections diagnosed in the entire United States. Also during the previous decade, Massachusetts was the only state reporting even a single case of the disease in all of New England. Still more shocking was the knowledge that this epidemic in Vermont, in the spring of 1968, was North America's largest outbreak of tularemia on record linked to human contact with aquatic mammals. In fact only one, a tick-borne epidemic in Tennessee in 1943, had been larger.

Investigators determined that 70% of the infected muskrats had been trapped along Dead Creek, the rest in descending order, had come from Little Otter Creek, Lemon Fair River, Otter Creek, and Lewis Creek. The infection spread over an area 12 latitudinal by 15 longitudinal miles, or 180 square miles. At Dead Creek, 9 out of 10 people who had handled muskrats that spring contracted tularemia, and it was here that authorities recovered the tularemia organism from mud samples taken directly from the walls of an abandoned muskrat house, and from the surrounding water. This supported the theory that the infection of the animals occurred orally by the waterborne route.

The human victims had become infected through direct contact with the carrier muskrats. Many of these people had cuts, scratches, or other skin lesions on their hands and had handled the animals without wearing gloves. Others did not show evidence of skin lesions and initially this led some officials to disagree with the diagnosis. But the ability of the tularemia organism to penetrate unbroken human skin has been reported. Blood tests later confirmed that the disease was indeed tularemia.

A large ulcer developed over the left eyebrow of one man who frequently wiped his brow while skinning animals. Interestingly enough, of three persons who handled more than 50 animals taken from Dead Creek but who remained well, two wore gloves while skinning, and a third hired two skinners, both of whom had become ill. None of the fur dealers who handled only dry pelts became infected, but one fur dealer who had handled still moist pelts was stricken.

The severity of the illness varied considerably and, while there were no fatalities, several of the 47 victims were incapacitated for periods ranging from five weeks to four months. Symptoms included *hectic fever* (one that is attended by a continuous and exhausting drain upon the human system), skin ulcers, chest pain, swollen lymph glands, and were generally flu-like.

None of the findings of the investigations give any clue as to why tularemia suddenly occurred in an area where cases had never been seen before. It was noted that smaller outbreaks were reported simultaneously in New York and Ontario, and in Quebec rabbit-associated tularemia was reported at the same time – for the first time in 35 years.

Officials concluded that two hypotheses seemed reasonable. The first, supported by the fact that the region along upper Dead Creek is a large bird sanctuary, was that migratory birds had contaminated the water. It is documented that the tularemia organism may be carried by birds and excreted in their feces. The second hypothesis was that the water had been contaminated by a widespread infection of field mice. If this had occurred near the headwaters of the streams and creeks, it might have resulted in a concentrated, waterborne dissemination of the organism.

Tularemia is a word I cannot recall having heard as a young boy growing up on a farm in Milford, then a small town in Massachusetts southwest of Boston. But I have vivid memories of a playmate that, bedridden, lost several months of school because of a mysterious illness. His father, an avid hunter, frequently brought home game birds, venison, and rabbits for the family dinner table. One of those rabbits was stewed with vegetables and served one ill-fated evening, and a few days later my friend was stricken.

The doctor traced his problem to the rabbit stew. Apparently the meat had not been thoroughly cooked. The illness was diagnosed as *rabbit fever,* and my friend nearly died. That was 1951, more than half a century ago. Just one year later, Selman A. Waksman (1888-1973), an American microbiologist, was awarded the Nobel Prize for his discovery of the antibiotic streptomycin in 1943. Had it not been for Dr. Waksman, my friend may not have recovered.

The disease was first described in 1911 by scientists studying a plague-like illness in ground squirrels in and around Tulare County, California, hence the name tularemia. By 1928 Edward Francis, an American bacteriologist, incriminated rabbits as one of its most important hosts and he established transmission via deer flies. Because of his work most texts refer to the bacteria as *Francisella tularensis,* though it is also known clinically as *Pasteurella tularensis.*

Lee Foshay (1896-1961), another American bacteriologist, developed both a skin test and an antiserum for the diagnosis and treatment of tularemia before the advent of antibiotics which, as earlier noted, occurred during the 1940s. Foshay's skin test was a killed suspension of *F.*

tularensis, which was injected under the skin. An erythema (a spreading redness) developing at the injection site was viewed as a positive reaction. Foshay's antiserum was then administered, but only if the case was considered serious or life-threatening because this treatment frequently caused serum-sickness, an allergic reaction often resulting in severe shock and posing a threat to life in and of itself.

Modern diagnostic methods include various blood tests and, if *F. tularensis* is positively identified, the antibiotic streptomycin is still considered the treatment of choice. Continued research has also established that in addition to the deer fly other bloodsucking vectors, such as the tick and mosquito, transmit the disease from animal to animal, and from animal to human. We also now know that the tularemia bacteria occurs naturally in at least 48 species of vertebrates throughout North America, Europe, and Asia including rabbits, deer, squirrels, muskrats, mice, woodchucks, mink, rats, fox, coyotes, and skunks. It has been identified in various fowl, snakes, and fish as well. Not surprisingly, there is one case on record (JAMA 238:1845, 1977) attributed to the bite of a domestic kitten. However it usually concentrates its attack on, and is most prevalently found in hare, cotton-tails, jack-rabbits, deer, and their insect companions.

As one might expect of such a ubiquitous villain, tularemia, or rabbit fever, is known by other names in various parts of the country including *deer fly fever, tick fever,* and *O'Hara's Disease,* to name a few. They are all caused by the same bacteria, *F. tularensis,* a short, gram-negative, rod-shaped microorganism that does not produce spores, is non-motile, and is unaffected by exposure to oxygen. It's a member of the same family that gave us bubonic plague.

F. tularensis may enter human skin via an insect bite or a skin lesion usually on the hands and exposed while skinning or processing wild meat. It may also be ingested by drinking contaminated water, or consuming partially cooked venison or rabbit meat in particular, or it may be inhaled. The incubation period is typically from 3 to 5 days, but can range from 1 to 14 days. A victim might complain of severe headache, chills, nausea, malaise, diarrhea, and fever. If the bacterium penetrates the skin via an insect bite or an open lesion, the site of infection may become ulcerous. If consumed in under-cooked meat, ulcers may appear in the mouth. If inhaled, the victim may experience severe respiratory illness, including life-threatening pneumonia and systemic infection. In all cases, lymph glands may become enlarged, tender, and painful, and may even abscess. The victim usually perspires heavily and suffers rapid weight loss and debility. Inflammation of the eyes with itching, tearing, pain, and sensitivity to light is not uncommon. The disease can and has been confused with plague, Cat Scratch Disease, sporotrichosis (a skin and lymph node infection), ecthyma (a skin infection frequently associated with impetigo), and infectious mononucleosis.

The intensity of tularemia infection varies from mild to life-threatening. Before the advent of antibiotics, half of all victims who developed respiratory complications, such as pneumonia, died. Fortunately, Dr. Waksman's streptomycin, and in many cases gentamicin, are highly effective in treating the disease. Today, if the symptoms are recognized and properly treated, recovery is usually complete and generally confers immunity.

Tularemia is considered an occupational hazard for handlers of wild animal pelts. All who participate in dressing, skinning, and/or eating the meat of susceptible wild animals are at risk if the necessary precautions are not taken. To a lesser degree, everyone exposed to the bite of a deer fly, tick, or mosquito is vulnerable. But the disease is not believed to be transmissible from person to person.

Many cases of tularemia have been traced to contaminated water. Since the disease cannot be eradicated in the wild rodent population, sportsmen, especially those in areas known to be infected, should avoid using streams for drinking water. Waterborne epidemics have occurred in this country and in Eastern Europe. In the final analysis however, most references indicate that rabbits are the most common culprits associated with human infection accounting for up to 90% of all cases diagnosed in the United States.

Tularemia has now been reported in all U.S. states except Hawaii, and in the District of Columbia. About 200 cases are reported in the U.S. annually, most occurring in the south-central and western states. In the summer of 2000, on the island of Martha's Vineyard off the coast of

Massachusetts, 15 cases were confirmed and one of the victims died; the first confirmed tularemia death in the state since 1996. The Martha's Vineyard Times reported on May 26, 2009, that from 2000 through 2006, there were 59 cases of tularemia associated with the Vineyard, more than in the previous 50 years. Of those, 38 were tularemia of the lung, according to state Department of Public Health (DPH) officials. A public health study conducted in 2000-2001 found that people on Martha's Vineyard with pneumonic tularemia most likely got sick by breathing in contaminated dust, soil, or grasses while brush cutting, lawn mowing, or doing other similar landscaping activities. Dr. Bela Matyas, medical director of the DPH epidemiology program, said it appears that there are animals involved in the transmission that do not play as important a role elsewhere. In particular, skunks and raccoons show a high rate of infection and face no pressure from natural predators. Their droppings and carcasses could also play a role in the high rates.

A typical contact case occurred on November 15, 1977, when a 19-year-old King County resident went deer hunting with friends and relatives in central Washington state. Along the hunting trail he found a partially dismembered, dead rabbit, and amputated the animal's front paws for good luck charms, which he then gave to another hunter in the party. The 19-year-old who found the rabbit had handled the carcass with bare hands, which were bruised and scratched from his work as an auto mechanic. Four days later, sores festered on his hands, legs, and knees. Twenty-four hours later he spiked a fever. He was cared for at home until December 11 when, nearly a month after exposure, he was admitted to a local hospital due to continued fever and weight loss. Tularemia was diagnosed, yet the person he had given the infected paws to reported no ill effects.

The CDC in Atlanta, Georgia, developed a tularemia vaccine in the 1960s to protect high risk laboratory workers, but it was never commercially available. Currently a live vaccine strain is under investigational new drug status by the U.S. Army Medical Research Institute at Fort Detrick, Maryland, but several limitations indicate a need to move forward with the development of improved vaccines. Aerosol dispersal is considered the most hazardous mode of transmission but despite the increased risk of a bioweapons threat felt after 9-11-2001, further vaccine development for tularemia remains slow.

The National Institute of Allergy and Infectious Diseases (NIAID), part of the National Institutes of Health, announced in 2005 that it had made several dozen awards to further strengthen the nation's biodefense and emerging disease research capabilities. The new awards include grants for two five-year contracts totaling approximately $60 million to support the development of a vaccine against tularemia, a potential agent of bioterror.

Widespread immunization against tularemia may never be commercially practical or medically advisable. Nonetheless, this much is certain, humans are incidental but highly susceptible hosts. While the *F. tularensis* fatality rate is comparatively low, infection is at best temporarily debilitating and the bacterium has proven that it can kill. Twenty deaths in the United States between 1985 and 1992 have been attributed to *F. tularensis* infection and stand in mute testimony to that fact.

As with other naturally occurring threats to humankind, which abound in the heavily populated world around us and elude the naked eye, prevention is always the safest and surest cure. Fellow hunters might laugh when you put on rubber gloves to dress or skin a rabbit or a deer, but you might find some consolation in the fact that they could be the fools.

BRUCELLOSIS

(UNDULANT FEVER)

The Norman (Oklahoma) Transcript published an editorial by syndicated news columnist Baxter Black in September of 2008 advocating the wholesale slaughter of roughly 30,000 elk and 3,500 buffalo in Yellowstone National Park, which is located primarily in Wyoming but extends into Montana and Idaho as well. Black argues "Since 1934 the U.S. has depopulated (slaughtered) hundreds of thousands of cows as part of the Brucellosis (eradication) program", and goes on to claim that the elk and buffalo herds in Yellowstone Park represent "the last wasp nest of infection".

Kurt Repanshek, publisher and editor of the National Parks Traveler, responded in disbelief: "Now, the newspaper doesn't mention that domestic cattle transmitted brucellosis to the park's elk and bison in the first place. And it doesn't touch on the elk and bison in nearby Grand Teton National Park. Nor does it detail how such a killing program would be carried out. After all, many of the estimated 30,000 elk that summer in Yellowstone also disperse into the surrounding forests in Montana, Idaho and Wyoming. How would anyone know when all the brucellosis-infected elk are dead?"

It's a volatile issue among livestock owners and naturalists, as one might expect, and there's no simple answer in sight. In terms of animal-to-human transmission, however, much progress has been made. There were 6,321 human cases recorded in the United States during 1947, but according to John M. Sauret, M.D., of the State University of New York at Buffalo, today there are approximately 100 human cases reported nationally each year with most reports originating in Texas, California, and Illinois. The CDC's estimates are somewhat higher, confirming that while human brucellosis is not very common in the U.S., there are still 100 to 200 cases reported annually. Worldwide, however, more than 500,000 new human cases are reported each year with most originating in countries that do not have good standardized and effective public health and domestic animal health programs, most of which are located in the Mediterranean Basin, South and Central America, Eastern Europe, Asia, Africa, the Caribbean, and the Middle East.

Brucellosis is an infectious disease caused by the bacteria of the genus *Brucella*. Various *Brucella* strains affect sheep, goats, cattle, swine, dogs, deer, elk, caribou, reindeer, wild boar, bison, and other animals. One strain also affects harbor seals, porpoises, and certain whales. The bacterium usually causes infected animals that are pregnant to abort, but otherwise animals generally appear to be symptomless, though they continue to harbor the organism intracellularly. Animal-to-animal risk factors include breeding, nursing, infected food supplies, and contact with aborted fetuses. There is some suspicion that the bacteria might also be spread by bloodsucking insects such as ticks but there is little discussion of this in current literature.

Humans can be infected in three ways: by ingesting something that is contaminated with *Brucella*, inhaling the organism, or access to the body through skin wounds. Hunters in particular may be infected through skin wounds or by accidentally ingesting the bacteria after cleaning infected deer, elk, moose, wild boar, or other susceptible wild animals that they have killed.

The spread of brucellosis from person-to-person is extremely rare but can occur. Mothers who are breast-feeding may transmit the infection to their infants, and sexual transmission has also been reported.

In humans, brucellosis can cause a range of symptoms similar to the flu that may include fever, sweats, headache, back pain, and physical weakness; miscarriage; and in some cases, severe infections of various organs have occurred. Although the disease is commonly non-specific, suggesting a generalized infection, in about one-third of patients the infection is localized or confined to a specific area in the body. The most common sites for localization are the joints (osteoarthritis), genitals (orchitis), brain (encephalitis), heart (endocarditis), central nervous system (meningitis), or liver (hepatitis). Occasionally the *Brucella* bacteria will localize on foreign material in the body such as artificial joints or pacemakers. Brucellosis can also cause long-lasting or chronic symptoms that include recurrent fevers, joint pain, and fatigue.

Treating brucellosis can be difficult. Usually, antibiotics such as doxycycline and rifampin are used in combination for 6 weeks to prevent reoccurring infection. Depending on the timing of treatment and severity of illness, recovery may take a few weeks to several months. Mortality is low (less than 2%), and is usually associated with endocarditis. Long-term immunity following infection is uncertain.

Brucellosis is also commonly referred to as *Undulant fever*. The term originates from the characteristic wave-like nature of the fever, which rises and falls over a period of weeks in untreated patients. In the 20th Century, brucellosis and undulant fever gradually replaced the 19th Century names *Mediterranean fever* and *Malta fever*.

The disease was first described by British medical officers in Malta during the Crimean War in the 1850s, but the fact that it was caused by an organism wasn't recognized until 1887 when it was studied by Dr. David Bruce, a Scottish pathologist and microbiologist, who was stationed in Malta while serving with the British Army Medical Service. A decade later, Danish veterinarian Bernhard Bang isolated *Brucella abortus* as the responsible organism and the affliction also became known as *Bang's Disease,* which is often referred to simply as *Bangs* by ranchers.

In 1954, a strain of the *Brusella* bacteria was the first agent weaponized by the United States at the Pine Bluff Arsenal in Arkansas due to its ability to survive well in aerosols and resist drying. These and all other biological weapons in the U.S. arsenal were reported destroyed in the early 1970s when the U.S. offensive biological weapons program was discontinued. The Public

Health Assessment of Potential Biological Terrorism Agents prepared by the CDC, classifies *Brusella* as a Category B bacteria while *Anthrax,* a much more serious bacteria, is listed in Category A.

While no method guarantees the prevention of brusellosis, hunters handling animal carcasses should always wear gloves, particularly if they have open wounds or lesions on their hands. Careful hand washing is paramount after the handling of an animal carcass or raw meat. And the meat of wild animals in particular that are susceptible to infection should be thoroughly cooked.

ROCKY MOUNTAIN

SPOTTED FEVER

According to the CDC, Rocky Mountain Spotted Fever (RMSF), caused by the bacterial organism *Rickettsia rickettsii,* is the most severe tick-borne rickettsial illness in the United States. It is found throughout the United States, except in Maine, Alaska, and Hawaii. Despite the name, few cases are reported from the Rocky Mountain region. More than half of all cases occur in the southeastern United States, particularly in North Carolina and Oklahoma, which alone account for about one-third of the total number of cases reported annually. In 2003 and 2004, more than 1,800 cases were reported each year, nearly five times the 365 cases reported in 1998. The reasons for this increase are not known, but wide swings in the incidence of RMSF have occurred since 1920. Generally, there are 250 to 1,200 cases reported annually in the United States.

The name, *Rocky Mountain Spotted Fever,* is a misleading misnomer as less than 2% of the total number of cases are found in the Rocky Mountain states. The disease was named after the Rocky Mountain Laboratories, a facility of the National Institute of Infectious Diseases, in Hamilton, MT, where much of the early research was conducted. RMSF was first recognized in 1896 in the Snake River Valley of Idaho and was originally called *black measles* because of its characteristic rash. It was a dreaded and frequently fatal disease that affected hundreds of people in this area and by the early 1900s, the recognized geographic distribution of the disease grew to include parts of the U.S. as far north as

Washington and Montana, and as far south as California, Arizona, and New Mexico.

Before 1875, the Salish or Flathead Indians living in the Bitterroot Valley of western Montana ate the bitter roots of a pink spring flower as a medicine. They ground the roots in a mortar and pestle and made a medicinal porridge or tea, and named the river and the valley after the plant. The Salish showed no evidence of the illness that affected subsequent occupants of the valley, but the Indians knew about the disease. Investigators Michie and Parsons reported in 1916 an elderly Indian told them that every year in the spring-months, evil spirits occupied the canyons west of the Bitterroot Valley (Lo Lo Canyon, a notorious site of infection).

Research on the disease began around 1900 in the Bitterroot Valley of Western Montana. Early settlers were plagued with a deadly disease of unknown origin and folk wisdom of the day suggested that infection occurred from drinking the melted snow water that gushed out of the west side canyons during spring run off. Fatal in nearly 4 out of 5 adult cases, local residents appealed to the state governor for help.

Montana had been granted statehood in 1889, and when the Montana State Board of Health was created in 1901, its first priority was to bring health scientists to the Bitterroot Valley to investigate. One of the first was Dr. Howard T. Ricketts, a pathologist from the University of Chicago, who proved the disease was transmitted by the bite of the Rocky Mountain wood tick. The organism was later named in his honor. Tragically, Dr. Ricketts died of typhus, another rickettsial disease, in 1910 while working in Mexico.

The classic triad of findings for this disease is fever, rash, and a history of tick bite, with the rash having a *centripetal*, or inward pattern of spread, meaning it begins at the extremities and spreads towards the trunk. Following an incubation period of 5 to 10 days after a tick bite, initial symptoms may include fever, nausea, vomiting, muscle pain, lack of appetite, and severe headache. Later signs include the rash, abdominal pain, joint pain, and diarrhea.

Because *R. rickettsii* infects the cells lining blood vessels throughout the body, severe manifestations of this disease may involve the respiratory, central nervous, gastrointestinal, or renal systems, and victims are usually hospitalized. Long-term health problems following acute infections include partial paralysis of the lower extremities; gangrene requiring amputation of fingers, toes, or arms or legs; hearing loss; loss of bowel or bladder control; movement disorders; and language disorders. These complications are most frequent in persons recovering from severe, life-threatening disease, often following lengthy hospitalizations. Overall, RMSF is fatal in 3% to 7% of cases. However, it is fatal in over 30% of those who are not treated. The mortality is higher in people over 40 years of age. Death usually results from shock and kidney failure.

An outbreak of the disease that occurred between 2002 and 2004 and killed two of 16 infected patients in rural eastern Arizona has been traced to the common brown dog tick, not generally recognized as a vector. The two patients who died from the infection did not initially receive doxycycline because the disease was not suspected or was not diagnosed early enough. For the 20-year period from 1981 to 2001, only three cases were reported in the entire state of Arizona, where the usual tick vectors are rarely found.

Victims treated five or more days after the onset of symptoms experienced three times the mortality rate of patients treated earlier. Long-term morbidity is most usually seen in patients in whom treatment has been delayed. Those who died received antibiotics an average of two days later than those who lived. Whites have twice the incidence of African-Americans, however, the latter have a higher case-fatality rate, perhaps due to greater difficulty recognizing the rash in highly pigmented individuals. American Indians are at greatest risk.

It is now known that the bacteria are transmitted to humans by three different types of ticks: *Dermacentor variabilis* (American dog tick) in the eastern states, *Ablyomma americanum* (Lone Star tick) in the west south central states, and *Dermacentor andersoni* (wood tick) in the western states. RMSF is responsible for more deaths than any other tick-borne illness in the United States. There is a case fatality rate of up to 30% in untreated patients. Approximately 612 people died of the disease between 1983 and 1998. On the bright side, infection with *R.*

rickettsii usually provides survivors with long-term immunity.

BORRELIA (LYME DISEASE)

According to the CDC, Lyme disease is the most common vector-borne disease in the United States. In the span of eight years, from 1990 through 2007, a total of 292,930 cases were reported nationally. The disease is considered endemic in 10 states including Connecticut, Delaware, Maryland, Massachusetts, Minnesota, New Jersey, New York, Pennsylvania, Rhode Island, and Wisconsin. Of the 27,444 cases reported in 2007, 23,859 or 87% were in these 10 states. Case figures for 2008 won't be published until August of 2009. Cases occur most commonly in the northeastern, mid-Atlantic, and north-central states, and among persons aged 5-14 years and 45-54 years. Since Lyme disease became nationally notifiable in 1991, the annual number of reported cases has nearly tripled.

In November of 1975, the Connecticut State Health Department (CSHD) received a phone call from two mothers who lived in the small town of Lyme. Each reported that her child had been diagnosed with juvenile rheumatoid arthritis, and each knew of other children in the area with similar symptoms. It is a very serious illness, and is extremely rare in children. The news alarmed state health officials and CSHD contacted Dr. Allen Steere who was studying rheumatology at New Haven's Yale University.

In a relatively short period of time, Steere and his colleagues identified 39 children and 12 adults suffering from juvenile rheumatoid arthritis. The number was astonishing because the disease normally affects one child in 100,000. It was also determined that the outbreak was confined to three Connecticut townships on the east side of the Connecticut River: Lyme, Old Lyme, and East Haddam. And it was noted that most of the victims lived in heavily wooded areas.

Dr. Steere concluded they had discovered a previously unrecognized disease, which was probably viral in nature and most likely transmitted by an anthropod (insect, spider, or tick). Initially Steere called it *Lyme arthritis,* but the name was changed to Lyme disease when it was confirmed that the infection affected the heart and nervous system as well as the skin and joints.

In 1981, during a totally unrelated investigation, live *Ixodes* (deer) ticks were collected on Long Island, New York, and sent to Montana's Rocky Mountain Laboratories where a fatal case of Rocky Mountain Spotted Fever was being studied. While working on this case, entomologist Willy Burgdorfer, an international authority on tick-borne diseases, isolated new spirochetes belonging to the genus *Borrelia* from the mid-guts of the deer ticks, and he showed that they reacted with immune serum from patients previously diagnosed with Lyme disease. The new etiologic agent was named *Borrelia burgdorferi,* in honor of it discoverer.

B. burgdorferi is transmitted to humans by the bite of infected ticks belonging to certain species of the genus *Ixodes* (the hard-bodied *hard ticks*), but transmission is relatively rare with only about 1% of recognized tick bites resulting in Lyme disease. This may be due to the fact that an infected tick must be attached for at least a day for transmission to occur. Congenital transmission can occur from an infected mother to her fetus through the placenta during pregnancy. The risk of fetal harm is much higher in the first three months of pregnancy. Prompt antibiotic treatment almost always prevents fetal harm.

Early symptoms of infection may include fever, headache, fatigue, muscle-soreness, depression, and a characteristic skin rash called *erythema migrans,* which is a red, circular, outwardly expanding rash that appears at the site of the tick bite 3 to 32 days after being bitten. The rash may be warm, but is generally painless. Classically, the innermost portion of the rash is dark and appears to harden, the outer edge remains red, and the portion in between may clear, giving the appearance of a bullseye, though the partial clearing is uncommon and occurs in fewer than 10% of all cases. The incubation period from infection to the onset of symptoms is usually one to two weeks, but can be much shorter (days), or much longer (months to years).

BORRELIA (LYME DISEASE)

Left untreated, complications can occur involving the joints, heart, and nervous system. In most cases, the infection and its symptoms are eliminated with oral antibiotics such as doxycycline, amoxicillin, or cefuroxime axetil. Patients with certain neurological or cardiac forms of illness may require intravenous treatment with drugs such as ceftriaxone or penicillin. If patients are treated with antibiotics in the early stages of the infection, they usually recover rapidly and completely. But some patients, particularly those diagnosed with later stages of the disease, may have persistent or recurrent symptoms.

After several months, untreated or inadequately treated patients may develop severe and chronic symptoms affecting many organs of the body including the brain, nerves, eyes, joints, and heart. Other serious symptoms can also occur, including permanent paraplegia in the most extreme cases. Lyme arthritis usually affects the knees, but in some patients arthritis can occur in other joints including the ankles, elbows, wrist, hips, and shoulders. Pain is often mild to moderate, usually with swelling at the involved joint(s).

A vaccine was developed by GlaxoSmithKline and approved by the Food and Drug Administration (FDA) in 1998, but hundreds of people who were vaccinated reported they had developed autoimmune side effects. These claims were investigated by the FDA and the CDC and were determined to be without merit, but lawsuits were filed and sales plummeted, prompting GlaxoSmithKline to withdraw the product from the U.S. market in 2002.

Most cases of human Lyme disease occur in the late spring and summer when the ticks that carry it are in the nymphal stage and are most active, and human outdoor activity is greatest. Although the ticks often feed on deer, these animals do not become infected, but they are important in transporting ticks and maintaining tick populations. The Lyme disease bacterium, *B. burgdorferi*, normally lives in mice, squirrels and other small animals.

Patients who have removed a tick often wonder if they should have it tested. In general, the identification and testing of individual ticks is not useful for deciding if a person should get antibiotics following a tick bite. Nevertheless, some state or local health departments offer tick identification and testing as a community service or for research purposes. Check with your health department; the phone number is usually found in the government pages of the telephone book.

CDC Web Site

Department of Health and Human Services

Centers for Disease Control and Prevention

http://www.cdc.gov/ncidod/dbmd/diseaseinfo/default.htm

How to Avoid Ticks

When in tick infested areas (tall grass, overgrown brush, wooded areas), the CDC recommends the following:

- Wear light-colored clothing.

- Tuck your pant legs into your socks.

- Wear closed-toe shoes.

- Use commercial insect repellent with no more than 20% - 30% DEET.

- Use repellents sparingly and with care as they may cause side effects, especially in young children.

- Avoid applying repellent to damaged skin.

- When returning from any outdoor activities it is important to check yourself, your children, and your pets for ticks. Carefully inspect all joint areas, the navel, the groin, behind the ears, in the hairline, and in other skin folds.

- Wash all skin treated with inspect repellent thoroughly.

How to Remove Ticks

Ticks should be removed as soon as possible. The CDC recommendations for the safest tick removal are as follows:

- Use tweezers to grasp the tick as close to the skin surface as possible.

- Pull up on the tick with slow, even pressure to gradually ease out the tick's mouth parts.

- If tweezers are not available, use fingers shielded with tissue paper or rubber gloves.

- **Do not** handle ticks with your bare hands.

- **Do not** use petroleum jelly, nail polish remover, or heat to remove the tick as these methods may increase the risk of infection with a tick-borne disease. The use of flame, a burning cigarette, or other heat sources may actually make matters worse by irritating the tick and stimulating it to release additional saliva or regurgitate gut contents, increasing the chances of transmitting the pathogen.

- **Do not** squash or squeeze the tick during removal.

- Wash the area of the tick bite, and your hands, with soap and water after the tick is removed.

- When outdoors, especially in tick-infested areas, check for ticks attached to clothing or skin every 2 to 3 hours.

About the Author

Jerry Genesio was employed by Cutter Laboratories for almost 20 years. For most of that time he was an account executive in Cutter's Biologicals Products Division, which specialized in biological products derived from human blood through a process called fractionation. He has written and published numerous articles, including a natural history series focusing on zoonotic diseases. Jerry lives in Bridgton, Maine, and Wilmington, North Carolina.

www.ingramcontent.com/pod-product-compliance
Lightning Source LLC
Chambersburg PA
CBHW060640290526
45793CB00001B/331